MW00834641

DISCOVERING AMERICA
★ An Exceptional Nation ★

Work, Exchange, and Technology in the United States

Cassandra Schumacher

Cavendish Square

New York

Published in 2019 by Cavendish Square Publishing, LLC
243 5th Avenue, Suite 136, New York, NY 10016

Library of Congress Cataloging-in-Publication Data

Names: Schumacher, Cassandra, author.
Title: Work, exchange, and technology in the United States / Cassandra Schumacher.
Description: New York : Cavendish Square, [2018] |
Series: Discovering America: an exceptional nation |
Audience: Grades 7-12. | Includes bibliographical references and index.
Identifiers: LCCN 2018021288 (print) | LCCN 2018024771 (ebook) |
ISBN 9781502643612 (ebook) | ISBN 9781502642622 (library bound) |
ISBN 9781502643605 (pbk.)
Subjects: LCSH: United States--Economic conditions--Juvenile literature. |
United States--Economic policy--Juvenile literature.
Classification: LCC HC103 (ebook) | LCC HC103 .S378 2018 (print) |
DDC 330.973--dc23
LC record available at https://lccn.loc.gov/2018021288

Editorial Director: David McNamara
Editor: Caitlyn Miller
Copy Editor: Rebecca Rohan
Associate Art Director: Alan Sliwinski
Designer: Joe Parenteau
Production Coordinator: Karol Szymczuk
Photo Research: J8 Media

Printed in the United States of America

★ CONTENTS ★

Christopher Columbus arrived in the Americas in 1492 with a fleet of three ships: the *Niña*, the *Pinta*, and the *Santa Maria*.

Chapter One

Working Toward a New Nation: 1491 to 1800

I n the fall of 1492, Europeans landed on the shores of the so-called New World. Sailing at the behest of King Ferdinand, Italian explorer Christopher Columbus sought wealth and fortunes from China and India (the Indies) in the name of Spain. These Asian cultures held wealth in gold, spices, and silks. The voyage west was slow and dangerous, requiring travelers to navigate around the African continent and the dangerous waters of the Cape of Good Hope at its tip. Seeking a western route, Columbus hoped to shorten the trip and believed, incorrectly, that traveling east rather than west would accomplish this. He never made it to China.

On August 2, 1492, Columbus set sail for the Indies and instead, on October 12, found himself on a continent previously unknown to his contemporary Europeans. Though early Viking voyagers had reached North America centuries before, Columbus is credited with the "discovery." The lands were already inhabited by people with rich culture and heritage. The word "discovered" is therefore misleading—if not outright inaccurate. Nonetheless, Columbus's expedition is credited as first contact.

Columbus did not realize that he had not reached the Indies. Knowing only what he had read from voyages of other explorers, Columbus had little knowledge of what India and China looked like. Encountering Native Americans, he found people that he deemed "uncivilized" from their differences in dress, mainly because they wore less clothing than the Europeans.

Then he found gold. Combined with Caribbean beaches, it was enough to convince him he had made it to Asia. He was actually in the Caribbean, most likely San Salvador. From there, he voyaged to the islands of modern-day Cuba as well as Haiti. Columbus was convinced he had reached Japan and other Asian lands. In Haiti, he claimed the island for Spain, created a village with thirty-nine men, and called it La Navidad. Columbus dubbed the island Hispaniola. The island was already occupied by the Taíno people, but Hispaniola would become known as the first American colony.

From there, Columbus returned to Spain with enough gold and captives to "prove" he had found the Indies. He would return three more times but never fully understood what his initial voyage would mean for the world at large. First contact with the New World had been made, and it would change everything.

The Conquistadores

Following Christopher Columbus's 1492 voyage, European powers took a great interest in the New World. The sixteenth century was marked by the continued contact between Native American populations and Spanish explorers and invaders. Known as conquistadores, these explorers and conquerors included Hernán Cortés in the Aztec lands of Mexico in 1519; Francisco Pizarro in Inca-controlled Peru in 1531; Sebastián de Bencalcázar in 1533 and Gonzalo Jiménez de Quesada in 1535, both in what would become Colombia; and Pedro de Valdivia in Chile in 1541. These men invaded with armies and guns, and they took hold of large cities from Native leaders. They came for gold, slaves, and riches, and stayed to develop colonies.

The military campaigns into the New World created immense wealth for the invaders. The leaders of the expedition could expect 20 percent of the wealth harvested, the Spanish king was given 20 percent, and the remainder

The brutal conquistadores were met with resistance. This painting by Emanuel Leutze depicts the Aztec defense of Tenochtitlan against Hernán Cortés.

was given to the troops. Precious gems, gold, silver, and clothing were some of the wealth and commodities the conquistadores received. Wars were fought between the Native populations and the conquistadores, but it was far from a fair fight. The Europeans had guns and disease where the Native populations did not. The conquistadores wrested control from the Native leaders in a brutal fashion. Afterwards, the Spaniards created the *encomienda* system to maintain their control.

The *encomienda* system (meaning "to entrust") granted conquistadores control over the lands they invaded. The idea was that conquistadores and other wealthy Spaniards would rule the New World lands and populations. The Native populations were to work the land for the Spaniards in exchange for protection and European goods. The reality was that the Native populations were enslaved and abused. It was an oppressive system and indicative of the general relationship that would develop between the Native Americans and European invaders. The cultural exchange between Europe and the Native New World is known as the Columbian Exchange.

The Columbian Exchange

The Columbian Exchange was the cross-cultural exchange between the New World and the Europeans during the sixteenth century. Its impact is singular in global history. As a result of Columbus's discovery, the conquistadores, and the *encomienda* system, a large-scale intercontinental exchange of goods, ideas, and disease took place. The Columbian Exchange had an astounding impact. The items and ideas that were brought to and taken out of the New World would change human history forever. Everything from plants and animals to technology and resources was shared and traded, some intentionally and others merely as a result of contact.

Technology

Contact between the New World and Europe resulted in the exchange of language, steel, guns, and farming practices. The New World gained a written alphabet. Native populations learned about metal goods like plows, which made farming easier. Gunpowder and guns were also a defining characteristic of the European presence in the New World. Having guns and gunpowder (discovered in the 1300s and 1400s) helped the Europeans invade and overthrow Native populations in the New World.

Plants and Animals

Plants traded as part of the Columbian Exchange included chilies, flowers, and maize. One of the most influential vegetables was the potato, which was easy to grow and enabled the European population to grow rapidly. Potato cultivation led to a surplus in high-calorie food stores, which were used to feed a growing population. Other New World crops included—but were not limited to— peanuts, tomatoes, and squashes, such as pumpkins. Grains like wheat and oats were exchanged alongside cabbage and lettuce. Goods like tobacco and cocoa became cash crops and commodities that Europeans coveted. Increased farming of other cash crops like sugar and coffee swelled global supplies of both.

Domesticated animals like pigs, turkeys, horses, cattle, sheep, and goats came from Europe into the Americas. In return, the New World provided animals like llamas and birds. As a consequence of the animal trade, the fleas, ticks, and bacteria that lived on the animals were also exchanged. Bacteria and diseases would have the greatest impact of all.

Disease

The most detrimental exchange came in the form of disease. There is some evidence that diseases like syphilis and tuberculosis came from the New World, but far more came from Europe. It was disease that truly made it possible for the Europeans to colonize the Americas because it had a catastrophic effect on Native populations. Illnesses like smallpox, malaria, whooping cough, chicken pox, influenza, typhoid, cholera, yellow fever, measles, and plague decimated Native populations who had no immunity to the illnesses. Europeans, on the other hand, had dense populations with high levels of animal domestication. These factors led to high rates of disease— as well as increased immunity to those diseases. Native American communities were more spread out and relied much less on domestication. Therefore, there were far fewer diseases as well as much lower immunity to them. Diseases like smallpox and measles ran rampant in the New World. It is estimated that within one hundred years of European contact, about 90 percent of the Native population in the New World was killed. It was genocide by disease. The remaining people were enslaved.

Slavery and Labor

The Europeans were partially drawn to the New World for the free labor of enslaved Native American people. Thanks to guns, steel weaponry, and disease, Europeans were able to enslave whole populations. The flaw of this plan, excluding the tragedy of slavery, was that disease drastically reduced the Native populations. Europeans were forced to rely on the African slave trade to compensate for the Native deaths. Ultimately, this unpaid labor force gradually pulled European nations from feudal societies into capitalist societies.

In a feudal society, a lord owned a large plot of the land called a fief. The fief was farmed by serfs, who were poor and of a lower class. The serfs rented the land from the lord by giving him a portion of their crops. The lord then sold or used the crops and added to his wealth. However, with a slave economy, the feudal system was no longer needed. The unpaid labor provided by enslaved people created surpluses that could be turned into goods that were sold in open, free markets. This meant there was more money with which to experiment and create new technology and to produce new products. Over time, this excess wealth created new markets.

Competition within those markets led to a capitalist system. Furthermore, there was now a surplus of food. New crops, like the New World's potato, were higher-calorie foods with higher yields. There was more food to feed a larger population, which led to a population boom. More people also translated to more money spent overall. The rising dependence on cash markets decreased the need for feudal protection and land sharing. With that change, it became more valuable to colonize other lands—especially the New World—rather than to maintain the feudal system.

These widespread economic changes all came to fruition because of slavery, which was possible because of the *sistema de castas*—a racial caste system. A caste system is when social status and class are determined at birth by race or wealth. In the Spanish colony of Mexico, caste was decided by race and skin color. It was used as a means to justify European rule over Native and African populations. It was also a prime example of a racist system.

Colonial Technology

The Spanish presence in the Americas was followed by the arrival of other Europeans. The seventeenth century was defined by colonialism, which was made possible

In the *sistema de castas*, Spanish-born Europeans were the highest caste. They were the fewest in number but had the greatest amount of power and wealth. Known as the *peninsulares*, this caste was the ruling class and the only caste that could hold positions of power. Below the *peninsulares* were the creoles, who were Europeans born in America. This caste could own land but not serve in high-level government or church positions. They were followed by the mestizos. The mestizo caste consisted of the children born of a European parent and a Native American parent. The existence of this class was a direct result of Spanish colonists intermarrying with Native people.

Mulattoes were the caste below the mestizos and comprised the children from European and African unions. Zambos were the offspring of the Native people and African people. Finally, the Africans were the enslaved people brought over to the New World to work. They were the lowest caste.

By segregating people into castes, the Spanish were able to create the plantation system that would define and shape American politics and society far into the future. Slavery and exploitation began with the very first settlers and would continue well into American history. All the while, there was wide cultural exchange throughout the world at large due to the exploitation within the New World.

Seafaring ships such as these were used to navigate the Atlantic Ocean during the fifteenth century as a way of colonizing the New World. They relied on wind for power.

by new developments in technology. In order to achieve intercontinental travel, the Europeans used a thirteenth-century Chinese invention to determine direction: the compass. Tools like a clip log, invented in the sixteenth century, helped a navigator determine their speed in knots, which were literal knots tied into the string that was attached to the clip navigator and hung overboard. Transverse boards helped explorers track their path, a crucial skill when traveling in open water with no land in sight to mark movement. Other tools like portolanos, which held what amounted to sailing directions, also helped navigators cross the oceans. Combined with tools for determining longitude and latitude, seafaring became a possible and fruitful endeavor.

Changes to ships themselves were most essential to European success during colonization, however. Europeans began building longer, faster, and sturdier ships during the fourteenth and fifteenth centuries. These new ships were able to survive the long trips across open waters like the Atlantic. Having a larger ship made with a sturdier body allowed voyagers to hold their own against rough waters and storms, increasing the chances of successful crossing. Larger ships also allowed for more supplies to be carried between the Americas and Europe, which made survival more likely and facilitated the Columbian Exchange.

Europe and Colonization

Following the Spanish occupation and colonization of Central America was a huge influx of other European powers into the New World. These powers arrived during the sixteenth and seventeenth centuries and parceled out the land of the New World for their own economic gain. Gaining land meant more resources and power, and European entities commandeered that land with little regard for the Native populations already living there.

New France was established around the Saint Lawrence River in 1534, and the first French settlement was founded in Quebec in 1608. French territories would ultimately span from parts of modern-day Canada down to Louisiana.

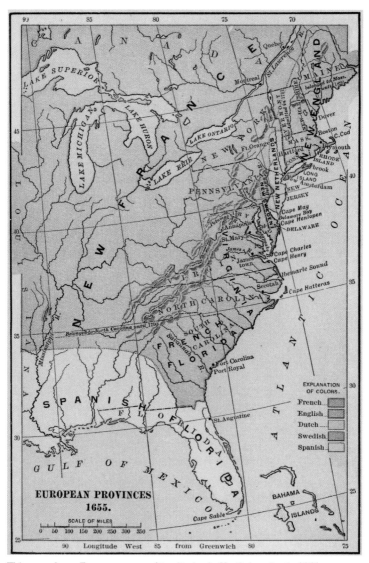

This map shows European powers' territories in North America in 1655.

In 1585, the first English colony was formed on Roanoke Island in North Carolina. The venture failed and became the "lost colony" after its residents disappeared—perhaps having deserted the island. In 1607, the English tried again, this time in Jamestown, Virginia. Eventually, they would have holdings along the East Coast all the way down to the top of what is now Florida. The English also controlled northern portions of Canada.

Through the exploration of Henry Hudson in 1609, the Dutch focused their energies farther north in what is now known as New York. Called New Amsterdam, the Dutch founded the first settlement on today's Manhattan Island, and Dutch territory traced up the Hudson River.

As time progressed, the Spaniards in the south began to expand north into modern-day Texas. They also moved into the southwest and established interests in modern-day Florida. Between their territories in South America and North America, Spanish holdings in the New World were sizeable.

A Look at the Colonies

Different countries had different goals for their colonies, but the ultimate goal of colonization was to increase wealth for the home country. The end of the feudal system and movement into the capitalist market meant greater interest in trade—locally and internationally. This created a middle class that dealt largely in commerce and trade. Motivated to find new resources and goods to buy and sell, European nations branched out through exploration. From there, colonies became new sources of revenue as well as goods and raw materials. The old adage that "money is power" rang true. Countries needed income and revenue to fortify their power. The more colonies a nation had, the more sources of revenue they created. Colonies also increased the number of markets in which to sell and trade.

Spain was strongly driven by economic gain. The conquistadores came seeking gold and stayed to create the *encomienda* system, which provided free labor for harvesting raw materials and goods. Crops like tobacco and sugar were valuable, but Spain did not leverage the New World markets well. By merely profiting off of the goods that could be taken from the New World, the Spanish were not able to set up colonial trade patterns that would have led to longer-term, more sustainable wealth. This was not true of other European nations.

Though the Spaniards found gold in South America, North American colonialization had its own riches: fur. One of the major motivators of the French presence in the New World was the fur trapping and trade down the Saint Lawrence River. Eventually, beavers would be hunted and trapped into near extinction through the French fur trade. The beavers' pelts were used to fashion clothing and accessories, especially the felt hats that were very popular with the wealthy.

The early fur trade revolved predominantly around Native people. Native Americans would hunt the animals and sell and trade the furs to early French and English traders. In return, the Native people received commodities like guns and goods like cloth. Then, the traders returned to their home country to sell the pelts. These furs turned a substantial profit.

The English also took part in the fur trade as well, though to a lesser extent than the French. The English and Dutch were seeking more effective long-term economic gain from their colonies than either the Spanish and French had. They used so-called joint-stock companies to help fund their colonialism. Joint-stock companies are funded by multiple investors who own parts of a company and collaboratively provide money to fund a venture—in this case, colonies.

In Holland, the Dutch had the West India Company to fund their colonialism. In 1624, the first effective Dutch colony began on Manhattan Island. Two years later, the West India Company sent Director General Peter Minuet to purchase the island from the local Native Americans and found New Amsterdam. Under his guidance, the colony went from a fur trade–focused economy into a more diversified economy that included more agriculture.

Each of Great Britain's colonies had unique characteristics and provided different resources to the mother country.

The British Colonies

The British also raised funds through joint-stock companies but focused their colonies on farming. With a stronger focus on agriculture, the colonies were able to become more individually sustainable. They were ultimately money-making ventures, though some were driven by religious freedom. Jamestown and Maryland, founded in 1607 and 1632, respectively, were centered around tobacco farming on plantations.

The Puritans founded Plymouth in 1620, and Massachusetts in 1629 for religious freedom; the Puritans were also farmers. However, the depth of the Puritan piety varied, and other colonies would later be created as sects branched off. A pious group founded Connecticut, which merged with New Haven in 1633. The more lax Puritans created Rhode Island in 1636. New Hampshire also arose around this time.

In 1664, the Dutch lost their colony to the English. New Amsterdam, which was founded forty years earlier, was renamed New York. Delaware started as a Swedish colony, came under Dutch and then British rule, and was eventually worked into a British land deal with Quaker William Penn along with Pennsylvania, which became a Quaker safe haven in 1682. New Jersey was divided into two charters that would eventually be united into one colony in 1702. Farther south were farming colonies. Carolina was established in 1670 as an agricultural colony, producing cotton, rice, and indigo on plantations. Georgia came later, in 1732, and produced rice.

Ultimately, all of the colonies produced exports for England. The northern colonies were sources for fish and whale products like oil, as well as lumber, maple syrup, and fur, among other riches. The middle colonies supplied wheat, corn, and livestock, as well as lumber, coal, textiles, and ships. The southern colonies were farming hubs and provided goods like cotton, indigo, sugar, rice, and tobacco. They were also the primary sites of plantation-based farming.

Unrest

The colonies flourished under the British crown for years. Colonists were comfortable with the general guidance and basic control the monarchy wielded. The colonists formed local governments and traded with the British. Eventually, with ever-growing colonies and populations, tensions with the Native Americans mounted and conflict broke out. This tension was exacerbated when France and Great Britain came into conflict over empires in the New World. As a result, the Seven Years' War, more commonly known as the French and Indian War, began in 1754.

The French allied with Native American tribes that they were familiar with through trading. The British allied with the Iroquois (more appropriately referred to as the Haudenosaunee). The French, alongside their numerous allies, were winning until William Pitt took over control of British forces and fortified their troops in 1756. Ultimately, the British triumphed over the French. Peace came in 1763 and involved the British gaining control of significant territory in the Mississippi Valley. However, the war also created a huge deficit in the British coffers. War was expensive, and this one had left the British deeply in debt. To make up for the cost, the British turned to the colonies.

Seeking to pay off the debt accumulated during the French and Indian War, the British turned to the American colonists. As the debt was created because of the colonists, it seemed to the British that the colonists must help pay it off. Taxes were levied on nearly all paper products and legal documents. Everything from playing cards and dice to wills and deeds as well as every notarized document was taxed. The colonists were livid. The following is an excerpt of the act:

> *Whereas by an act made in the last session of parliament, several duties were granted, continued, and appropriated, towards defraying the expences [sic] of defending, protecting, and securing, the British colonies and plantations in America: and whereas it is just and necessary, that provision be made for raising a further revenue within your Majesty's dominions in America, towards defraying the said expences [sic]: we, your Majesty's most dutiful and loyal subjects, the commons of Great Britain in parliament assembled, have therefore resolved to give and grant unto your Majesty the several rates and duties herein after mentioned.*

Taxation

After years of very little British intervention in American trade and business, the tides had changed. For years, taxes had gone unpaid, and colonists even began printing their own money. After the French and Indian War, the British began taxing American colonists in earnest. The new changes were not received well. The colonies instantly protested.

Rather than roll back the taxes, the British passed the Currency Act in 1764, which stopped the printing of colonial paper money. This made it so that taxes and debts had to be paid in British pounds. Then came the Stamp Act, levied in 1765. This British tax was on paper products as well as legal documents. Documents needed a government stamp to be binding (hence the name). The colonies reacted violently. Virginia's local government, the House of Burgesses, legally forbade the British from passing such legislation over the colonists. Boston colonists ransacked the stamp distributor's house, and the protests spread like wildfire.

The colonies unified to fight the tax in October of 1765 and petitioned the British Parliament to say that parliament did not have the right to tax American colonists. The idea of "no taxation without representation" was born. To underscore the petition, Americans began boycotting

In 1773, the Sons of Liberty boarded the East India Company's trading ships and upended crates of tea into the Boston Harbor.

British imports, and the English government was forced the repeal the tax in 1766.

The repeal was followed by the passage of the Declaratory Act in 1766, which reinforced British rule over the colonies, and eventually the passage of the Townshend Acts a year later, which taxed many items like tea, glass, paint, and paper again. The colonists rioted. Their resistance was met in 1770 with the Boston Massacre.

Tension between the colonists calmed somewhat until the 1773 passage of the Tea Act. The act favored the British joint-stock company the East India Company. The company was granted a monopoly on the import and distribution of tea to the colonies. This had a huge impact on colonial markets, where tea was an important commodity. The colonists protested passionately against the Tea Act. In December of 1773, a group of Boston colonists called the Sons of Liberty took their revenge by boarding East India Company ships and dumping 342 chests of fine British tea into the Boston Harbor. The load was worth $1 million in modern currency.

The British crown brought down the full weight of the law in 1774. The Coercive Act, grouped with the Intolerable Acts, was a swift and brutal punishment. The new laws stipulated that only British officials could decide verdicts in court, suspended the Massachusetts local government, closed the colony's port, gave land to France that the colonists wanted, and enabled British soldiers to enter and board in any colonial residence they chose to be in. The colonists' fury over it all fueled the American Revolution.

Protest and defiance broke out and raged for two years, ending with the Declaration of Independence in 1776. Under the guidance of General George Washington, the Continental Army managed to triumph over the much stronger and richer British army during the war. In 1783, with the Treaty of Paris, the Americans won their freedom.

The antebellum period, or the period before the Civil War, was marked by conflict over slavery.

Chapter Two

Under Construction: 1800 to 1877

★ ★ ★ ★ ★ ★ ★

At the close of the Revolutionary War, Americans had to determine what their nation would look like in a rapidly changing world. The start of the nation coincided with industrialization, which was quickly changing European society. The country experimented with implementing democracy, building a capitalist economy, and industrializing in rapid succession. The United States of America was under construction.

The Founding Fathers and New Nation

In 1781, the Articles of Confederation created the federal government that was put in place after the Revolutionary

★ ★ ★ ★ ★ ★ ★

War, but the document was not enough to sustain the nation. Though the states had unified to defeat the British, the Articles showed how loosely they were tied. Designed to have a weak central government, the states had significantly more power under the Articles than they should have had. The federal government was not strong enough to broker trade with international entities or to regulate trade internally. Furthermore, the government had neither an executive branch to control and enforce laws, nor a court to execute and interpret them. The federal government was too weak to lead the nation, something that became increasingly evident as time passed. The depression during the 1780s showed the new nation was floundering.

A new system was necessary, but what the federal government should look like was a point of contention. The Founding Fathers struggled to come to a consensus about how the country's government and economy should be structured. James Madison and Thomas Jefferson formed the Democratic-Republican Party, maintaining that the primary focus of the new government should be westward expansion and agrarian (farming) interests. They believed that markets should be heavily driven by agriculture, and manufactured goods could be imported from Europe. This model did not encourage the industrial growth taking place in England that was making its way to American shores. The Republican view was the preference of the majority of the country.

In the other camp was Alexander Hamilton, a member of the Federalist Party. Hamilton was more in favor of growing into a more industrial model. His focus for the country was economic growth and development primarily through manufacturing. He saw the country as becoming a strong, international power with a very strong industrialized economy. Where Madison and Jefferson looked for visual growth of the country in size and space, Hamilton wanted a market that would be sustainable longer term and help the country move into the future rather than stay as it was.

Under Hamilton's model, the new country would move strongly into the capitalistic, industrial model that was growing ever-popular in England thanks to the Industrial Revolution. As Hamilton became the first Secretary of the Treasury under the new government, it quickly became apparent who would win the battle. America industrialized.

Industrialization in the Budding Nation

To understand the end of the eighteenth and the start of the nineteenth century requires a study of industrialization. The Industrial Revolution started in England during the early part of the 1700s. By the time America was declaring independence, the Industrial Revolution was well underway. It was the beginning of a new era—the

This view of Lowell, Massachusetts, shows a series of textile mills lining the Merrimack River. Mills used the flow of the river for power.

era of the manufacturer. Characterized by incredible growth in technology and the rise of mechanized labor, the Industrial Revolution was rapidly changing society. Mass production enabled the production of manufactured goods at an unprecedented rate, creating new markets and new income. The middle class grew, as did the working class and poor. It was a new era unlike any before, and it all began with fabric.

The textile industry was the first to reach America. Brought from England by Samuel Slater in 1789 as memorized and stolen plans from British factories, textile factories began appearing along American waterways. Textiles drove the new American markets. Thanks to the factories and inventions like the spinning jenny and the cotton gin, textiles were dramatically shaping American society.

Work, Exchange, and Technology in the United States

The spinning jenny was invented by James Hargreaves in 1764. The machine spun wool into yarn at a very fast rate. The cotton gin was even more consequential when it was invented by Eli Whitney in 1794. It changed the American economy dramatically by quickening the practice of separating cotton from its seeds. Thanks to this invention, cotton became one of the most valuable cash crops that could be grown.

Slavery in America

Slave plantations growing cotton became increasingly popular as a direct result of the cotton gin's invention. Plantations consisted of large farming enterprises that often focused on a single cash crop in mass production. They were farmed using slave labor. Due to the decimation of the Native populations, the early Spanish settlers had begun bringing African slaves into the Americas to work their lands. This continued in British colonies as well. With the rising demand from textile manufacturing for increased cotton output, more slaves were brought into the country as a free labor source.

At the writing of the Constitution, it appeared that slavery was gradually dying off. The first voices of resistance really began to be heard, but because it seemed that the end of slavery was near, it was left out of the Constitution.

Slave ships were cramped, hot, and deadly. Enslaved people received little food and water and were abused by slave traders.

No one anticipated the dramatic rise of the importance of cotton that followed. According to historian Gene Dattle, "in the first half of the nineteenth century, cotton was primarily responsible for the enslavement of four million African Americans."

Treatment of slaves was inhumane and abusive. Of the Southern population prior to the Civil War, one-third of the population were enslaved Africans and African American decedents. Enslaved people were not allowed to learn to read or write, nor could they marry. They were physically and sexually abused. They could be whipped by the slave owner or overseer or even punished with burning and mutilation.

Work, Exchange, and Technology in the United States

Slaves were forced to work incredibly long hours and were not treated with basic human decency. American slavery was one of the most inhumane and unethical treatments of a population in American and human history. Racism fostered during this period would define American politics and social landscape for generations to come, even after the abolition of slavery. With the relationship between industrialization and cotton, it also created the American economy as it exists today.

The Constitution and the Economy

The debates on the new government between the Founding Fathers resulted in the Constitution of the United States of America being finalized in 1787. The new government vested more power in the federal government but balanced that power between three branches: the executive (the president), the legislative (the Senate and the House of Representatives), and judicial (the Supreme Court). By balancing the power between three branches, the Founding Fathers hoped to limit the control of each branch while also providing the strength necessary to unify the country. It worked.

States maintained many rights, but the federal government now had the ability to regulate interstate commerce and tax its people. National protection was in the hands of the federal government, and the ability to print money was a federal power. Finally, the document could be amended should the need arise. The first ten amendments to the Constitution are known as the Bill of Rights and protected citizens' rights from government interference and abuse. Under the Constitution, the rights of women and minorities were not addressed or represented until much later.

The Consequences of Industrialization

Textiles and the rising cotton market had begun industrialization in America, but they were only the beginning. Steam power was changing the way shipping and commerce took place. Steamboats were running on the major waterways in the first half of the nineteenth century, and railroads began stitching the nation together shortly thereafter. Railroads came into real prominence during the middle of the century, continuing into the twentieth century. During the nineteenth century, the nation was developing rapidly.

There was, however, a dark side to economic growth. The rise of factories also led to poor working conditions. Without labor laws, the primary concern of factory

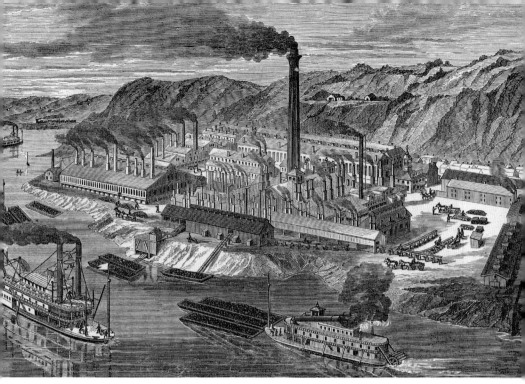

This iron works factory in Pittsburgh, Pennsylvania, was one of the many factories that sprang up during the Industrial Revolution.

owners was not employee well-being but making money. Factories were often dirty and dark. Every member of a family would have to work, including children. Because pay was so low, factory work required the participation of the full family to make a living wage. Children were even preferred as employees at times. For example, their small fingers were ideal for operating the finer points of machines. However, this preference was also because they could be paid less. Machines had few safety precautions and were dangerous to operate. The hours were long and the work often monotonous. Factories, however, moved the young nation of America into the nineteenth century as a growing economy. It was that new economy that led to the War of 1812.

War of 1812

Many historians consider the War of 1812 the second war for independence. France and Britain continued to battle for supremacy even after Britain surrendered her American colonies. Tensions in France were rising with the presence of Napoleon and festering political unrest. Americans were trading more with France as demands rose in light of wartime. Great Britain took great offense. Then, the French took offense to British offense. What followed was a large number of decrees and laws that resulted in neutral ships facing harsh consequences. If trading with France, the British navy would intervene. If trading with Britain, neutral ships would be intercepted by the French.

The British, however, took matters a step further. When the British navy would board American merchant ships, they would force sailors to join the British military—a process called impressment—claiming they were deserters. Thousands of men were impressed into the Royal Navy. This broke international laws and was an obvious challenge by the British to reassert control over the newly formed nation.

President Thomas Jefferson responded by limiting trade with England and pushing the Embargo Act through Congress in 1807. Under the Embargo Act, international trade slowed to a near stop. American merchants and ships were forbidden from trading in international ports. The US economy declined. Farmers had a surplus they could not move out of the country. Merchant traders stopped running large portions of their business. It was not sustainable, and smuggling rose as the US economy felt the pressure of the law. Two years later, Jefferson reopened ports to trade with nations other than France and England through the Non-Intercourse Act. Under James Madison, the fourth president of the United States, trade reopened with France through the passage of Macon's Bill No. 2 in 1810, which demanded that France and England allow trade with their opposition. France agreed, but resistance from England continued to intensify. In February of 1811, Madison forbade any trade with England.

Battle lines were drawn. England failed to recognize American neutrality and was treating the nation much like colonies rather than as an independent entity. Tensions with Native Americans on the frontier were increased by British occupation in Canada. The United States was at the brink of war. On June 1, 1812, the United States of America declared war on England.

Americans spent the following years battling British interests in Canada and their naval presence on the Atlantic. Britain, with its attention split between Napoleon in France and the United States, was stretched thin. The United States managed to wear them down until peace was declared on December 24, 1814, with the Treaty of Ghent. No one really won, and the treaty did not resolve the issues that led to war in the first place, but there was peace. Furthermore, British colonial interests were confined to Canada, and the American path to westward expansion was no longer impeded by British interests. It also finalized American independence from Great Britain.

Hamilton and Clay

Tariffs were definitive during the 1800s. A vast majority looked toward protecting the burgeoning US economy. Heavily dependent on cotton and seeking to protect manufacturing interests, the Tariff of 1816 limited trade with Britain after the War of 1812 ended. It was a part of the "American System" put forth by the Whig Party, most especially Henry Clay.

The American System was similar to Alexander Hamilton's original idea. Early on, Hamilton, as secretary of the treasury, had instated high tariffs to protect American imports and exports. To further defend American interests,

Henry Clay advocated for the "American System," an economic strategy defined by high tariffs.

he created the federal bank, the Bank of the United States in 1791. The bank managed federal funds; it was fairly conservative and slowed down economic growth but aimed at stabilizing the economy. It strongly drove manufacturing and industrial interests. The Republican mentality was driven by farming interests, so the bank was hated by Republicans. That said, industrial growth boomed under Hamilton's system. Trade was opened and closed several

Andrew Jackson is one of the most controversial historical figures in American history. He was the seventh president of the country and the leader of the Democratic Party. Jackson was a famed war hero for his efforts in the War of 1812 and also a staunch enemy of Hamilton's national bank. He referred to the bank as "the monster." This stems largely from his agrarian interests,

Andrew Jackson was the seventh president of the United States. His legacy is marked by his racism and his terrible treatment of Native Americans.

a direct contrast to Hamilton's support for industry and manufacturing. Firmly in the camp of states' rights, Jackson hated the power the national bank gave the government and spent most of his time as president attempting to undo what Hamilton had created.

Socially and politically, he was a supporter of slavery and the reason for the Trail of Tears with the passage of the Indian Removal Act during his presidency. As someone raised on the American frontier, he brought a different perspective to the White House. Strong, willful, and motivated, he exercised his right to veto and gained a lot of popular support for his efforts. He was both loved and loathed. He was also dependent on the spoils system, wherein he granted friends and supporters high-ranking positions.

Ultimately, while in office, Jackson targeted federal involvement in business. He stopped national charters that funded infrastructure. He worked to end the national bank by vetoing the charter and withdrawing all federal money from it. Additionally, he fed into the populist mentality that had gotten him elected by working to stop wealthy corporations. He attempted to give the people what they wanted: more land and money in circulation but at great cost. Jackson's policies, particularly the bigoted ones, left their mark on the economy—and people's lives.

times during the nineteenth century depending on the controlling party in the government.

Henry Clay, a congressman, senator, the Speaker of the House, and eventually secretary of state under John Quincy Adams, was hugely influential in the economic and political culture of the United States. Clay advocated for the American System. His American System was closely tied to the Hamiltonian era. High tariffs were meant to protect American interests globally as well as maintain the national bank. Clay had been an arbitrator in the Treaty of Ghent, and later his efforts in maintaining the Union and encouraging the economy on the road to the Civil War made him one of the most influential statesmen in United States history. His career shows the rocky nature and political environment of the country during the 1800s. Party lines and battle lines were being drawn, and at its heart was the issue of slavery.

Southern states were dependent on slavery to support their plantation system and economies. However, in the nation, dissent against slavery was rising. Abolitionists were calling for the end of slavery, but the nation was dividing over the issue. States had begun freeing slaves, and by 1819 when Missouri wanted to join the Union as a state, the division of "free" states and "slave" states was even: eleven free states and eleven slave states. Missouri wanted slavery. What resulted was the Missouri Compromise, in 1820. Under the compromise, Missouri was granted statehood as a slave state, and Maine was granted statehood as a free state. All territories below Missouri that were brokered as a part of the Louisiana Purchase would be entered into the Union as free states when the time came. Clay helped negotiate the Missouri Compromise, and the agreement stood for decades until the Kansas-Nebraska Act in 1854. Nonetheless, the nation was heading toward war at a dramatic speed.

Laissez-Faire Business and Regulation

Part of the reason there was so much contention over the business of slavery was that the federal government had a relatively laissez-faire (meaning "hands off") attitude toward economy and business. In a laissez-faire model, the federal government is relatively uninvolved in business. In the 1800s, there were tariffs passed and the national bank had some power, but business interests ran largely unchecked. Federalists and Whigs like Hamilton and Clay were pushing for greater government control and participation in business, while conservatives like Jackson were strongly driven to keep the federal government out of business interests. Decisions like freedom versus slavery were states' issues, but the political field was

In 1869, the first transcontinental railroad, the Union Pacific Railroad, was completed in Utah.

changing, and government intervention was becoming increasingly influential.

The country as a whole was growing rapidly. Westward expansion and industrialization were creating huge growth in the economy. With the tension caused

Work, Exchange, and Technology in the United States

by the coming Civil War, the United States faced a very volatile environment and was heading toward a shift in federal government. The government was becoming more involved in business, where before the capitalist free market of the American economy had gone unchecked and unregulated. A pivotal change in American history and the American economy was coming.

Steam, Trains, and Trade

The steam engine originated during the eighteenth century and revolutionized travel in the nineteenth century, but travel in general was an important step in American history—it allowed for manifest destiny. One of the key concepts of the eighteenth century, manifest destiny is a term first used by journalist John Louis O'Sullivan to describe the idea that it was the United States' destiny to span from the Atlantic Ocean to the Pacific Ocean. With the Louisiana Purchase in 1803, the purchase of Florida in 1821, and the annexation of Texas in 1845, the United States grew rapidly toward that goal.

An expanded nation fueled the need for new, innovative travel options. Achieving this goal started with the improvement of roads and the infrastructure of the country. In 1806, Congress funded a national road that ran from Maryland to Illinois. Cross-country trips by covered wagon and on horseback became increasingly common, and travel by water also grew more popular. The steamship was a new invention that allowed for faster and more efficient transport. Construction of canals, like the Erie Canal in 1825, also became popular. Even international travel increased and, combined with larger, more efficient shipping vessels, immigration increased. The real game-changer, however, was the railroad. The middle of the century was dominated by the construction and development of railroads that quickly stitched the North to the Midwest. The 1840s and 1850s saw a huge spike in railroad infrastructure, moving from 3,000 miles (4,828 kilometers) of track and increasing ten times over to 30,000 (48,280 km) within twenty years. By 1869, there was a transcontinental railroad that connected the country coast-to-coast.

The Civil War

Dramatic economic change, issues surrounding westward expansion, and contention over slavery came to a head in 1861 when the Southern states seceded from the Union. Republican Abraham Lincoln was elected in 1860 and took office in March 1861, and on April 12 of that year, the first shots of the war were fired.

The Confederacy consisted of eleven Southern states. Sympathy for the Confederacy was also found in Missouri,

Kentucky, and Maryland, though they remained in the Union. Looking at the Constitution of the Confederacy, it becomes apparent how economically driven the war was. Slavery was the foundation of the economy in the South. Political journalist Michael Lind says that the Confederate Constitution was essentially a rewriting of the United States Constitution with mercantile and industrial interests edited out. The South was looking to preserve their slave economy. What happened instead was four years of the bloodiest war America has ever known.

Contemporary technology of the era made it unlike any war prior and foreshadowed the destruction of later conflicts like World War I. Railroads and telegraphs meant supplies, troops, and information moved faster than ever. On the water, ironclad steamships battled for supremacy. More than anything, money was spent, and blood was spilled. It is believed that 620,000 soldiers died during the war. Families fought families, brothers fought brothers, and the country was ripped apart.

Telegraphs also ensured that Abraham Lincoln was informed very quickly of what was happening within the nation. Such information impacted his political moves. For example, he wrote the Emancipation Proclamation in the Office of the War Department while receiving live telegraph updates on the war. He also created the Bureau of Internal Revenue (this would become the Internal Revenue

Service) in 1862 as a part of the Treasury Department to help cope with the astronomical spending necessitated by the war. The Civil War created a $2.5 billion deficit, and taxes and treasury bonds helped pay for the costs. This was just in the North. By the end of the war, the South had spent $2 billion, the North $3 billion. Expert Michael Lind says at the end of the war, "two-thirds of southern wealth vanished."

The End of Slavery

The end of the Civil War in America created some of the most rapid social change to date. The Emancipation Proclamation of 1863 declared slaves in the Confederacy as free people. This did not extend to the northern states until 1865, when the Thirteenth Amendment was added to the constitution, outlawing slavery and involuntary servitude. The Fourteenth Amendment built on the Thirteenth by granting citizenship to freed people in 1868. The Fifteenth Amendment followed two years later, making it illegal to discriminate against voters, thereby enabling African Americans to vote. These amendments became known as the Civil War Amendments and sought specifically to protect the rights of the African Americans in the United States when the South rejoined the Union. At least four million enslaved people were freed.

The Fourteenth Amendment

The first section of the Fourteenth Amendment reads as follows:

Section 1.

All persons born or naturalized in the United States, and subject to the jurisdiction thereof, are citizens of the United States and of the state wherein they reside. No state shall make or enforce any law which shall abridge the privileges or immunities of citizens of the United States; nor shall any state deprive any person of life, liberty, or property, without due process of law; nor deny to any person within its jurisdiction the equal protection of the laws.

The amendment gave citizenship to all people born in the United States including African Americans. It also granted federal protection to African Americans, protecting them from state laws that could be detrimental. This law and the other Civil War Amendments changed American history dramatically and are still used today to defend the rights of American citizens.

Manhattan in 1900. The turn of the century saw a flood of Americans moving from rural areas into cities.

Chapter Three

Rebuilding and Growing: 1877 to 1945

★ ★ ★ ★ ★ ★ ★

The Civil War decimated the United States of America. Many young men had died, and the debt had ballooned. The country needed to rebuild infrastructure and the bonds of the Union. The nation was at a crossroads; citizens and the government had to determine what the reunified country would look like. The Reconstruction Era had begun and would last until 1877.

Reconstruction

Reconstruction saw vast changes in American society. Abraham Lincoln was assassinated at the end of the Civil War in April of 1865, leaving successor Andrew Johnson to determine how to move forward after the war. The

★ ★ ★ ★ ★ ★ ★

abolition of slavery and the passage of the Fourteenth Amendment had freed millions of people. These new citizens needed a place in society. The Confederacy needed to be reintegrated into the Union, and there were millions of dollars of debt and damage to rectify. As the name "reconstruction" suggests, the United States had to rebuild.

Those living in the South who pledged their allegiance to the Union were pardoned for seceding from the Union. The Southern states had to end slavery for good and reject secession permanently before they were reinstated and formed governments. Furthermore, these new governments were required to allow African American males to vote in elections. From there, the rest was in the states' hands.

Southern states responded to Johnson's mandates by passing racist laws that forced black workers to sign contracts in an attempt to reinstate the plantation system. These laws limited African Americans' working rights and were called black codes. Congress responded by passing the Freedmen's Bureau and Civil Rights bills in 1866, despite objections from President Johnson.

The Civil Rights bill ensured the legal protection and social standing of citizens regardless of their race, religion, or traits. The Freedmen's Bureau was more active and was designed to help people transition from enslavement to freedom by creating public services like schools and hospitals and granting them rations. However, it was undermined when Johnson returned Southern lands back to the Southern states. It was difficult to ensure fair treatment of African American people when there was no land for them to live on. The Southern landowners trapped African Americans into sharecropping land whereby, without land of their own, they were forced to work on the plantations where they were previously enslaved. It was exploitation and took advantage of the fact that the freedmen had few resources of their own.

Under the sharecropping system, African American families worked 20- to 50-acre (8- to 20-hectare) plots of land in exchange for a place to live, the use of the land, and the supplies necessary to farm it. The families would farm the crops that the landowner wanted, and the landowner would receive half the crop as payment for use of the land. The landowners charged high interest rates on goods, which perpetuated poverty. Though the sharecroppers had more autonomy and were free, the system still took advantage of them and acted as a form of systematic and overt racism to keep them disadvantaged and impoverished.

This injustice would be exaggerated by Jim Crow laws that segregated American society. Segregation, especially in the South, increased dramatically and divided public areas into black and white spaces. In 1896, the Supreme Court would hear and decide the *Plessy v. Ferguson* case, which questioned the constitutionality of the concept of "separate but equal" that was the foundation of segregation. The Supreme Court decided in favor of segregation, setting back civil rights progress by nearly one hundred years and ensuring the racist division of public spaces well into the twentieth century.

Farming and Industrialization

Even with the substantial death tolls of the Civil War, the United States population had been steadily rising. By 1870, there were forty million citizens. Common life expectancy was forty-five years old, and people worked hard during their lives. Farming was still a common practice even as it lost prestige, and people were moving westward for land. The rest of the country was moving toward manufacturing, and farmer unrest was growing. To protect and preserve their interests, farmers began forming cooperatives. Farming cooperatives worked alongside political parties like the Greenback Party of the 1870s. Farmers hoped that these cooperatives could lobby collaboratively to increase their political power and representation in government. Cooperatives had varied levels of success.

In the South, plantations had been destroyed by war, and the economic system of plantations had been stripped of its power. Even with sharecropping, profits were not near what they had been, and Southern goods like cotton were now competing with the same goods coming out of Egypt and India at lower prices.

By the 1870s, some Southerners began to push for a "New South," modeled after the industrial North rather than the continued dependence on old plantation methods. Seeing the failing infrastructure and economy, Henry Grady, an Atlanta news editor, said that formerly wealthy plantations should be broken up into more equal farms and that the economy should be diversified rather than remaining agrarian. Grady's idea never took off, and the South would suffer in the coming decades as poverty increased. Meanwhile, the North continued to develop and grow with the industrial model.

In cities, mechanized and factory labor was growing increasingly popular as well. The growing population and rise of factories led to a rising poor and working class—the primary laborers within the factory system. Where the South had stood still, the North experienced a renaissance. Though the economy and production declined after the war, new innovation was on the horizon that would fuel a revival. The Second Industrial Revolution was stirring with the promise of electricity, combustion engines, and the telephone. By 1880, all three inventions would be part of a changing America. The coming years would create an industrial boom that firmly and finally transported the United States into a manufacturing economy.

A Growing Nation

Westward expansion did not cease with the Civil War, and the United States continued to grow well into the twentieth century. New territories created new raw materials, and the growing size of the country created new markets. With the dawn of the Technological Revolution (spanning the 1870s to 1914), the country was tied closer together than ever before. Though the United States was still navigating the complex challenges of the post-war era, railways, canals, and other advances in transportation made for faster transport of people and goods than ever before. It was a landscape primed for industry.

Being able to reach ports and the Atlantic increased trade routes and options. With the added support of high tariffs

This map shows the movement of American interests during westward expansion.

instituted by the federal government, increased Native American relocation to allow for continued development, and a large store of natural resources, America was primed to grow as a force in global commerce. To encourage that growth, the government subsidized the development of railroads and gave land grants to them as well. Factories were erected quickly, and industrial goods began moving out of American ports.

The nation changed dramatically in a short thirty-year window. Steel, thanks to companies like the Carnegie Steel Company, became the foundation of American infrastructure. Skyscrapers began to define major cities. Kerosene, like that produced by John D. Rockefeller's Standard Oil Company, illuminated the nation, followed by electricity. Phonographs played music, and motion pictures amused Americans. By the 1890s, electric generators and electricity enabled Americans to enjoy the luxuries of refrigerators and washing machines. It was a completely different country than it was prior to the Civil War.

In 1913, with Henry Ford's development of the automobile assembly line, industry changed again. Prior to Ford's innovation, building a vehicle took twelve hours, but Ford's plants could produce a vehicle in just over an hour and half by 1924. Using assembly line production, Ford cut the costs of fabricating a Model T vehicle down dramatically to the point where many families could afford the luxury

Lewis Howard Latimer and the Light Bulb

B orn to two escaped slaves in 1848, Lewis Latimer was an African American inventor who worked with Thomas Edison and Alexander Graham Bell on two of the most influential inventions in modern history—the light bulb and the telephone. Latimer was an accomplished artist and would create the sketches for patents. Working with Bell, Latimer helped create the patent for the telephone.

After that, Latimer was hired at the Edison Company. With experience in patents and engineering, he was a smart hire. He even improved upon Edison's early model of the light bulb by creating a higher-quality carbon filament. He patented the filament as well as his production methods for creating it. From there, he continued to make other significant advances in lighting and electricity. His book, *Incandescent Electric Lighting: A Partial Description of the Edison System*, was one of the first ever published on the topic.

Lewis Howard Latimer was an African American inventor who contributed to the creation of the light bulb and the telephone.

Henry Ford's Model T was affordable and made travel by car a possibility for most of the American population.

at $260 (about $3,500 today). Mass production made fabrication simpler and faster by leveraging the assembly line. It also increased the quality of life for employees. With increased productivity, workers could work fewer hours and make a higher wage. It revolutionized industry.

The United States was becoming an economic superpower. The nation created one-third of the global industrial production in 1913. That was more than the total collective production of Germany, Great Britain, and France in the same year.

With industrialization, rural Americans began moving to cities. More than eleven million people relocated to urban centers during this era. That movement, combined with the continued influx of immigrants, had cities growing quickly and dramatically. The nation was now firmly an industrial, mercantile, and capitalist economy. With mechanization and industrialization, new markets were created and grew incredibly quickly. Industry was growing at dramatic rates, and so was the American economy.

Industrialization's Backlash

Alongside increased industrial success, there was dissatisfaction. The farmers' unrest that had started just after Reconstruction continued to grow. In the 1890s, the farm cooperatives continued to coordinate. From that community arose the Populist Party, which campaigned against Republican and Democratic political candidates. Droughts in the plains and on the prairie were making farming lifestyles increasingly challenging. International markets were making grain farming in the Midwest less profitable. Railroads and grain elevators set their own prices and made farming more expensive. Income was dropping from increased production. Finally, lenders were charging high rates for credit. Though not hugely successful because of dissent within the party itself, the Populist Party spoke about the increasing concerns that industrialization created for the traditional agrarian system. The group called for greater government intervention and regulation of the economy in order to protect farming interests.

Other voices also rose against industrialization. Unregulated industries led to injustice. Businesses were designed to make money and not with employee comfort in mind. The turn of the century saw increased social unrest over labor laws and workers' interests. The labor movement was born from the desire to improve working conditions. Unions had begun forming much earlier in the nineteenth century. Labor unions were organizations workers paid to participate in that protected the laborers' interests and rights. Unions could organize strikes during which workers would refuse to work until companies agreed to meet their labor demands. Strikes took place over wages, benefits, working conditions, and hours, as well as over other discomforts and rights violations. Calls for labor reform marked the early part of the twentieth century thanks to the Progressive era.

The Progressive era was marked by significant social change and advancement. Between 1890 and 1920, the Progressive era was a direct response to industrialization. With increased dependence on industrialization, quality of life decreased—especially for the working and poor classes. Progressives believed that government policy could be written for the good of the people.

Many of the journalists of this era were referred to as muckrakers. These social justice reporters dug through and exposed the dark and dirty parts of society in attempts to improve people's quality of life. Ida Tarbell tackled John D. Rockefeller's trust in oil by taking on the Standard Oil Company and its business practices in her 1904 book, *History of Standard Oil*. A trust is when a business owns every portion of the production and distribution of a product. This ownership enables that business to control the market. Rockefeller became a multibillionaire through Standard Oil. Tarbell's exposé brought the company's questionable and unethical actions to light and would lead to the Sherman Antitrust Act in 1890. The act anticipated Progressive President Theodore Roosevelt's trust-busting actions later on. Roosevelt would outlaw monopolies on markets and trusts on product creation that limited interstate trade and commerce.

Other media professionals were equally successful. Cartoonist Thomas Nast brought the political cartoon to American media with his cartoons criticizing political machines and dirty politicians during the late part of the nineteenth century. Writer and photographer Jacob Riis shed light on poor living conditions in New York City by exposing the state of slums and tenements in a photo series titled *How the Other Half Lives* in 1890. Lincoln Steffens's 1904 series of articles called "The Shame of the Cities" challenged political machines operating unchecked in cities around the country. These political machines were bribing government officials, leading to even more corruption.

"STOP THIEF!"
no sooner heard the cry, than, guessing how the matter stood, they issued forth with great promptitude; and, shouting 'Stop too, joined in the pursuit like *Good Citizens.*"—"OLIVER TWIST."

Thomas Nast's *Stop Thief! Boss Tweed and His Tammany Henchmen* political cartoon is critical of the people who knew of Tweed's corruption but failed to act.

Writer Upton Sinclair took on the meat production industry in his 1906 exposé, *The Jungle*. Essentially, Progressives began the movement of using social consciousness to encourage the government to regulate corporate action and social interests.

World War I

While the American economy was steadily growing, the rest of the world was growing more and more politically tense. International superpowers were allying. On June 28, 1914, the Austrian Archduke Franz Ferdinand and his wife were

I n this excerpt from *The Jungle*, Sinclair discusses just some of the revolting practices of the meat-packing industry in the 1900s. His work explains the unsanitary preparation

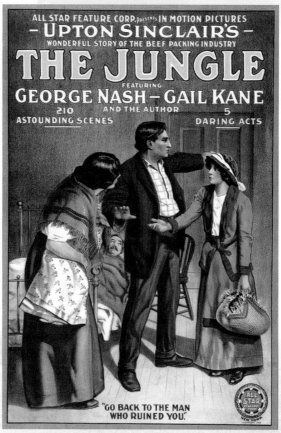

In 1914, Upton Sinclair's most famous exposé, *The Jungle*, was adapted into a movie of the same name.

practices but also included sections advocating for workers who worked in deplorable and dangerous conditions. Elizbieta, described here, is an immigrant working in one such plant:

> It was only when the whole ham was spoiled that it came into the department of Elizbieta. Cut up by the two-thousand-revolutions-a-minute-flyers, and mixed with half a ton of other meat, no odor that ever was in a ham could make any difference. There was never the least attention paid to what was cut up for sausage; there would come all the way back from Europe old sausage that had been rejected, and that was mouldy [sic] and white—it would be dosed with borax and glycerin, and dumped into the hoppers, and made over again for home consumption. There would be meat that had tumbled out on the floor, in the dirt and sawdust, where the workers had tramped and spit uncounted billions of consumption germs. There would be meat stored in great piles in rooms … and thousands of rats would race about it.

assassinated. World War I began. For the first years of the war, the United States remained neutral but not unaffected.

Almost immediately, US trade with Germany and Austria (the Central Powers) was interrupted by a British and French (Allied Powers) blockade. When the United States fought the blockade to continue trading as a neutral third party, the Allied Powers extended the blockade to include neutral nations. The German navy was even worse, attacking merchant ships with submarines. In May of 1915, the Germans sank the American ship, the *Lusitania*, destroying war goods and killing passengers. Germany gave in to President Woodrow Wilson's demands that submarines stop attacking ships without warning. Then, in 1917, they attacked again. As a result, Congress declared war, and the United States joined World War I.

World War I was a brutal, expensive endeavor. Fought in trenches and employing new technology like airplanes, tanks, artillery guns, and chemical warfare, World War I resulted in astronomical numbers of deaths on both sides. Though Americans were only at war for nineteen months, the war cost an estimated $32 billion dollars. Of the more than 4.7 million men who served, there were 116,516 deaths. An additional 204,002 were wounded. Worldwide, there were more than 65 million troops fighting; 8.5 million died and 21.1 million were wounded. The costs of the war took their toll on global economies. Nations were still paying off debt accrued during the war a century later. Crippling

Work, Exchange, and Technology in the United States

debt in Germany led to the rise of the Nazi party, which in turn would lead to World War II.

Between Two Wars

The decades between World War I and World War II in America were dramatic for their differences. The 1920s saw a huge rise in credit spending and diversified markets. Mass production ensured a surplus of varied goods, and credit was easy to come by. People were spending a lot of money. The rapid increase in new technologies and entertainments led to a booming, if highly unstable, economy. In an effort to shake off the horrors of World War I, American soldiers returned home to a decade known as the "Roaring Twenties." Filled with jazz, movies, and speakeasies, Americans were looking to have a good time.

The economy grew 42 percent in the 1920s. Infrastructure continued to grow as well. Europe was decimated by the war, so American production skyrocketed, producing about half of the entire world's output. The only market that suffered was farming, which continued to become less and less profitable. Everywhere else, wages jumped with the economic boom. People flooded into cities, and women earned the right to vote. Mass production increased access to luxury goods. Credit abounded. Lenders even let people use credit to buy stocks. The stock market seemed to be riding a rollercoaster that was only going up. However, buying stocks on credit would prove to be the American economy's undoing.

On October 29, 1929, the New York Stock Exchange crashed. Investors took huge, devastating losses. Known as Black Tuesday, that crash led to the loss of billions of dollars in a matter of hours. It had an impact so large it was felt around the world. The crash solidified one of America's most severe and devastating economic downturns: the Great Depression.

If the 1920s were a beacon of vitality, the 1930s were shrouded in debt and drought. Unemployment rose to an astounding 25 percent, and wages dropped by nearly half. The government tried to stabilize American foreign interests by passing the Smoot-Hawley Tariff and instead reduced world trade by 65 percent. The pains of the Depression were further exacerbated by a drought that hit the Midwest and created the Dust Bowl. Farming stood still. Not only were people poor, they were hungry, and Midwest farmers began making the pilgrimage to California in search of work. Impoverished people ended up homeless or camped in poorly constructed shantytowns, made from any materials that could be found.

It seemed that every move the government made increased the suffering rather than alleviated it. The dollar deflated, and the government would not print

Hoovervilles, like this one in Portland, Oregon, accommodated the rising homeless population during the Great Depression. The shantytowns were named after President Hoover, whom many blamed for the terrible conditions of the era.

more money to inflate it. There was a run on banks to pull out money, leaving an even smaller national supply of cash. Nearly hopeless, the nation turned to Presidential candidate Franklin D. Roosevelt and his wife Eleanor. Roosevelt was elected in 1932 because of his New Deal plan, which represented a new beginning that the nation desperately needed.

Roosevelt's New Deal was a series of public works programs designed to jumpstart the economy and get people back to work. People found jobs building infrastructure like dams, but the New Deal was not limited to building projects. Roosevelt passed many bills designed to bring life back into the economy. An example was the Emergency Banking Relief Act of 1933, which created presidential bank suspension in order to evaluate the national banking system. In 1934, the Gold Reserve Act took privately owned gold reserves and created a federal reserve at Fort Knox. Roosevelt also created new government agencies designed to alleviate the suffering of the American people. This was the origin of government administrations that are designed to provide funds for people out of work, like the Social Security Administration. Legislation was used as a tool to try to revitalize the economy.

Ultimately, it was not Roosevelt's New Deal that dragged America out of the Depression, however. It was World War II. It took an astronomical amount of spending to boost the economy again, and nothing is quite as expensive as war. On December 7, 1941, Japan bombed the American military base in Pearl Harbor, Hawaii, killing more than 2,400 soldiers and civilians. The following day, the president asked, and Congress declared war against Japan. America joined World War II.

World War II

As with World War I, the United States had attempted to remain neutral at the start of the war. President Roosevelt was focused on pulling the United States out of the Depression. The attack on Pearl Harbor made that impossible, and once again America found itself committed to a horrifying and expensive war. In four years, World War II cost the United States $296 billion, financed partially through taxes, bonds, and rationing.

Employment rates went up because of military spending. Manufacturing war goods created new industries and supported old ones. Men were drafted into the war, and women went into the work force. For the first time in more than a decade, America was spending enough money to keep the economy running. Propaganda sold the war effort at home, encouraging rationing of goods and resources.

By 1945, the war was over, the entire world was wracked with debt, and 1,076,245 American casualties had taken place. Globally, fifteen million soldiers died in battle, twenty-five million were wounded, and forty-five million civilians were killed. The world was shaken by the horrors of war, the injustice of the Holocaust and genocide, and the threat that nuclear warfare posed. It was a new world, one shaded by human horror and atrocity, and the United States was going to have to navigate being a global superpower among the wreckage.

The Cold War with the Soviet Union was a time of fear. Americans worried about atomic weapons and nuclear war. Propaganda like this advertisement helped promote American influence as a global superpower during the second half of the twentieth century.

Chapter Four

Modern America: 1945 to Today

A fter World War II, United States of America needed to find its way to an economy that relied less on manufacturing industries. Yet the economy was—and still is—defined by its combination of capitalism and democracy. Capitalism has had an incredible impact on the social and political culture of the nation. From the dawn of a new nation until the present day, the American economy has grown and changed, forming an exceptional nation dependent on capitalist markets and ideas. This was never so true as the years following the Second World War.

At the close of World War II, Americans raced European engineers to create an unforeseen threat. Through the Manhattan Project, the United States created the atomic bomb. Using nuclear fission, scientists created a bomb so explosive and destructive that it could wipe out whole cities and populations in seconds. Dropping two such bombs on Japanese cities ended the war. It also began a period of human history and American history filled with innovation forged in fear. The Cold War era had begun, and with it the quest to protect capitalism.

The Cold War Era

World War II ravaged Europe, destroying centuries-old architecture and infrastructure. The United States missed the wreckage as there was no front on the mainland of the country. Damage was done to American interests in the Pacific like Hawaii, but the nation did not have to focus on rebuilding infrastructure like Europe did. Instead, though in debt, American soldiers returned to a more financially stable economy than they had left.

More than anything, Americans wanted a return to normalcy. Women had maintained the home front and worked to supply goods for the war effort by staffing manufacturing plants. But it was a new world. Fear of communism and socialism continued to rise, threatening the American democracy and capitalism like never before. Chasing World War II was the Cold War era. Defined by the threat of nuclear war with the Soviet Union, decolonization, and incredible technological advances, this period laid the foundation for the modern economy.

Cold War Economy

Though the United States was not actively fighting, a large portion of the national budget was allocated to military spending during the Cold War. It would wax and wane throughout the forty years of the stalemated Cold War, though predicted attacks never came to pass. Neither the United States nor the Soviet Union wanted to directly engage. As both entities had nuclear weapons by this time, the threat of war was also a threat to the entire world.

Instead of direct warfare, the two superpowers fought through proxy wars, like the Korean War (1950 to 1953), the Vietnam War (1954 to 1975), and the Soviet involvement in Afghanistan during the early 1980s. The space race and space exploration were dominated by the desire to beat out the other nation so that neither the Soviets nor the Americans garnered the true upper hand. It was a stalemate between democracy and communism. Repeatedly, the two superpowers faced off, but shots were not fired. The technology that originated during this era had the power to destroy not only nations but the world, and political leaders on both sides understood the threat. However, both countries had to be diligent. Throughout the period, the United States government increased military spending as threats rose.

The Vietnam War was a Cold War conflict. The United States intervened in Vietnam, hoping to stop the spread of communism.

While the nation could not fight outright, the government turned to financial warfare like the trade embargo. In 1949, Congress passed the Export Control Act, which restricted trade with the Soviet Union and its allies. It compounded this move with the Battle Act in 1951, which refused aid to nations that did not embargo wartime goods to the Soviet Union. Though the Battle Act was not strictly enforced, and was therefore less effective, it showed how Americans were using the global market

Work, Exchange, and Technology in the United States

to control international politics. The Export Control Act remained in effect until the 1970s, when it was relaxed a little, only to be reinstated after the Soviet invasion of Afghanistan in 1979. There was a similar tight grasp on the trade embargo on China that lasted well into the 1970s, following their involvement in the Korean War.

The Cold War was fought through smoke and mirrors. Outright war meant decimation, but the United States sought to protect its global interest and democratic and capitalistic models. It was a tense era, where threats were around every corner and death loomed on the horizon.

Decolonization

Globally, the Cold War era saw an increase in decolonization. While the United States had been decolonized in the 1700s, much of Africa and other developing regions were still colonized until the twentieth century. Many colonized areas sought and found independence during this era. Powerful nations and entities like America were seeking global influence through decolonization and later by allying and influencing the development of budding nation states. Though America claimed that it was the first Western nation to embrace decolonization, the Cold War era saw an increase in American interference in developing nations. While not the outright colonization seen in European nations such as Great Britain in India and Africa, there is

Here the Prince of Wales, who would become King Edward VIII, takes a tour of African colonies in the early part of the twentieth century. European colonization of the African continent has had a lasting impact.

no way to deny that American interests drove the progress of developing nations toward democracy and capitalism. The United States was looking to protect its global interests and, as a world superpower, had the money and muscle to back up their demands. The Soviet Union, in turn, did the same by spreading communism.

Work, Exchange, and Technology in the United States

Counterculture

While the nation postured on the global front during the Cold War, fluctuating between periods of calm and decreased tension (détente) and high tension and threat, there was a shift happening within the borders of the

Hippies promoted social justice, love, and antiviolence. This famous photograph shows two hippies in San Francisco, California, in 1967.

Title IX was one of the liberal changes issued at the beginning of the 1970s that showed the changing culture. It outlawed any educational discrimination based on a student's gender. This increased women's access to educational services and extracurricular activities through educational institutions. More than anything, Title IX was driven by the absence of female sports teams. Now, under Title IX, a school or university must offer equal educational and extracurricular opportunities to all genders. It was an important step in educational equality for American citizens.

Title IX says:

Prohibition against discrimination; exceptions. No person in the United States shall, on the basis of sex, be excluded from participation in, be denied the benefits of, or be subjected to discrimination under any education program or activity receiving Federal financial assistance …"

United States. Generational divides were becoming increasingly clear. Counterculture impulses were rising among youth during the 1960s and 1970s, characterized by a resistance to the status quo.

While the government raged against communism, the counterculture at home raged against injustices present within the country. Based around liberal ideas of social justice, counterculture youth demanded civil rights for African Americans, raised interest in feminist and intersectional issues, sought to increase sexual liberation, and protested the Vietnam War. A large portion of this population was actively and at times violently protesting the war. Media made the war more present for civilians by broadcasting the ongoing events. That, combined with the purely political purposes for involvement, ensured that many people questioned America's role in the Vietnam War. The civil rights movement of the 1960s into the 1970s added to these factors to make the twentieth century an era of social change. It showed a shifting mentality in young populations. Older generations were often rooted in a traditional understanding of what family life should look like, a vision the younger generation was adamantly rejecting.

There were calls for greater government involvement in social justice and demands for a change in American culture as a whole. The result was increased spending on social programs, which raised taxes and led to increased government regulation on business.

Reaganomics

Many people had returned after World War II and desperately sought a return to normalcy by settling down and starting families. What resulted was a huge spike in population that put pressure on the economy then led to a boom in the economy. The "baby boomer" generation was born. Children born between 1946 and 1964 are baby boomers.

President Ronald Reagan is famous for a set of policies involving "trickle down"economics and tax cuts. His economic strategy is known as "Reaganomics."

During this period, more manufacturing took place, income levels rose, and the job market needed to expand as those babies grew up. Furthermore, there was a huge increase in immigrants arriving in the United States. From refugees from Hungary to Chinese immigrants seeking the opportunities believed to abound in the States, the large influx of immigrants into the country added further pressure on the economy. The 1940s and 1950s had been prosperous years, but the sudden population spike strained the economy. Combined with the demands for social growth and changing social and cultural structure of the 1960s and 1970s, the economy began to suffer. People started seeking and demanding a change that would meet the needs of the new population.

It was thereby that the radicalism of the 1960s and 1970s was met by a "watershed" election that defined the era, with a switch to conservatism through President Ronald Reagan. In what came to be known as Reaganomics, Reagan's conservative approach was characterized by tax cuts and decreased government regulations on the capitalist market hoping to alleviate the strain on the economy. Conservatives wanted to decrease government's presence in the economy, cut the liberal social spending on programs created under FDR's New Deal, and attempt to return to a more traditional model.

Reagan used top-down economics where the wealthy were granted huge tax breaks totaling 25 percent. The idea was that wealthy people would reinvest their saved income back into the economy, and the economy would stabilize. Reagan was trying to encourage the free-trade market by adding more money back into it. Instead, the national economy hit a recession in 1981 and 1982 that angered many people. The market did eventually stabilize as the tax cuts raised the value of the dollar internationally and raised interest rates, but it was a dramatic change from the more liberal economic model of the decades prior—especially as government funding for liberal social programs was cut.

However, Reagan's conservatism played out differently in reality than they did conceptually. During his presidency, Reagan did make tax cuts and spending cuts, but he enlarged the Social Security program once Congress refused to cut it. He pumped $165 billion into Social Security to keep the struggling social program from collapsing. This raised income taxes and led to the taxing of social security benefits. Reagan's strategies to save Social Security were followed with other tax increases to try to combat the debt and deficit the economy was experiencing. Reagan also increased military spending dramatically to bolster the military. Collectively, rather than solve the deficit as Reagan had planned, his actions compounded it. In 1981, the deficit stood at $90 billion. By 1989, it was at $255 billion.

Ultimately, what resulted from the fluctuations in the economy after World War II and during the Reagan years was a push to reform the financial systems.

The Twenty-First Century

Movement from the twentieth century to the twenty-first was marked by dramatic changes and growth in technology. These technological changes resulted in, and coincided with, economic changes as well. The population was also shifting south into a part of the country that historians call the Sun Belt.

It was a new millennium, and the markets were changing. Production costs led to outsourcing at the end of the twentieth century, whereby American companies would produce their manufacturing goods in plants outside of the United States to decrease costs. The increase in automation of production also added to the changes in the landscape of manufacturing. Taken together, these changes led to a shift in the market in the United States and decreased union participation. Fewer manufacturing jobs led to dependence on other markets, specifically the service market. Health care and social services became the foundation of the American economy at the beginning of the new millennium, and today the United States economy is a service economy. Change did not stop there.

Closing the Wage Gap

★

★

Today, social issues are a definitive factor in politics and the economy. Even with continued progressive change and social growth since the end of World War II, there is still definitive evidence of wage differences by gender and

Wage differences among men and women and racial and ethnic groups continue to be a problem today.

race. According to a 2016 report on full-time, year-round working women from the Institute for Women's Policy Research, women made an average of 80.5 cents for every dollar made by men. That is almost a 20 percent difference. For women of color, that wage gap is even greater. It is estimated that it will take until 2059 for Caucasian women to fully close the wage gap. For African American women, it will take until 2124, and for Hispanic women, it will take until 2233 if the rate of change follows the same trend it has taken for the last fifty years.

It should be acknowledged that, previously, women have gravitated to more service-based professions that tend to pay a lower wage than some of the technologically driven fields that drew men. However, that does not account for how dramatic the difference in earning potential is between genders.

Though strides have been made since the suffragists of the twentieth century gained the right to vote, advocating for women's and workers' rights is still necessary and important. Intersectional feminism, a modern form of feminism that is inclusive for minority women as well as transgender women and people of diverse backgrounds, continues to work toward equality for all men and women regardless of sex, gender, race, and ethnicitiy. The United States will need to close the wage gap in order to continue to work toward true equality for all genders and races.

Robotics are a key part of the manufacturing process at this General Motors plant.

Developments in technology led to increased dependence on technological assistance and dramatically increased access to news and media. Rising dependence on technology like cell phones and the internet connected society globally as well as locally in a way that was unprecedented. America was increasingly involved in global economics thanks to such changes in technology. Furthermore, new technology created new markets and increased economic spending and productivity. Digital media took over old markets and created new ways of sharing information. All this new technology directly impacted daily life and the economy in dramatic ways.

Despite the growth, development, and change, income remained the same. Since the 1980s, wages stagnated, or plateaued. The characteristic increases that took place in the century and half up to that point did not continue into the modern market—even though the cost of living continued to rise. It used to be that when productivity rose, so did wages. That growth was not present anymore. This changed the quality of life for people, most especially the middle class, the working class, and the working poor. The upper class continued to become richer and control the majority of the wealth while the lower classes increasingly struggled with the rising cost of living and stagnant earning.

Finally, people spent the early part of the twenty-first century moving to warmer climates. The growing trend in moving south changed the political impact and power of states in the Sun Belt. This belt includes states like Florida, Georgia, and the more western states that get a lot of sun, including Texas and all the way to Southern California. The population shift toward the Sun Belt greatly impacted politics. The population shift changed government representation because increasing populations led to more congressional representation. Sun Belt states gained political power and influence, and the new populations led to an increase in business and industry. Furthermore, immigrants from Central and South America continued to build a growing Latinx population. Combined

The Sun Belt is shown here in red. As people move to the Sun Belt, demographics shift and so do voting patterns.

with increased immigration from Asian countries, the demographics of the nation were changing the economy and political environment. Continued debate of how to handle illegal immigration was a key issue in the 2016 presidential election.

A Coming Generation

As the millennial generation moves into their late twenties and early thirties, Generation Z is close behind. The digital developments during the last twenty years ensure that the society and economy of coming generations could be vastly different from those that existed previously. As a nation founded on a democratic capitalistic model since colonial times, those changes are sure to have an interesting impact on coming generations and the economy. Technological advancement does not appear to be slowing down, and it has the potential to impact the future economy dramatically as well. Even within the last twenty years, the service economy in place currently is different from the mercantile and manufacturing economy that dominated the United States' markets for more than one hundred years. What this new market will look like in ten, twenty, even one hundred years in the future is dependent on the new generation.

It is hard to deny that in light of increasing changes in social and political policy, America could look quite different from its current form as this coming generation grows up into adulthood. Some economists forecast tragedy; others see a bright future. The truth most likely lies somewhere between the two, but it is ultimately in the hands of these rising generations to determine what the United States will look like in the coming years. These young people are inheriting a model where a majority of the wealth is in the hands of very few people, one where a wealth gap is growing ever larger between classes, and one where a technological boom is redefining society in a way similar to the Industrial Revolution in the nineteenth century. How the rising generations choose to combat and solve economic problems will define the future of the nation. Young people hold the country's future in their hands.

★ CHRONOLOGY ★

1492 Christopher Columbus lands in the Caribbean Islands on an island he dubs Hispaniola.

1585 England attempts to establish a colony, Roanoke, in North Carolina, but the colony disappears.

1607 England forms its first successful colony, Jamestown, in Virginia.

1754 Fighting breaks out between French and English forces in the Ohio River Valley, beginning the French and Indian War (Seven Years' War).

1763 The French and Indian War ends.

1764 British Parliament passes the Currency Act; the spinning jenny is invented.

1765 British Parliament passes the Stamp Act.

1766 British Parliament repeals the Stamp Act and the Declaratory Act.

1767 British Parliament passes the Townsend Acts.

1770 The Boston Massacre results from protests and rioting in Boston.

1773 The Tea Act is passed by British Parliament. The Boston Tea Party takes place in protest of the Tea Act.

1776 The American Revolution begins.

1781 The Articles of Confederation are ratified.

1783 The American Revolution ends with the Treaty of Paris, and the United States becomes an independent nation under the Articles of Confederation.

1787 The Constitution of the United States of America is written.

1791 Secretary of the Treasury Alexander Hamilton creates the National Bank.

1794 The cotton gin is invented.

1803 The United States of America buys the Louisiana Territory from France.

1806 Congress builds a national road from Maryland to Illinois.

1807 Congress passes the Embargo Act.

1810   Macon's Bill No. 2 is ratified.

1811   America ceases trade with England.

1812   The War of 1812 begins.

1814   The Treaty of Ghent ends the War of 1812.

1820   The Missouri Compromise goes into effect.

1825   The Erie Canal is completed.

1830   Andrew Jackson passes the Indian Removal Act, which forces thousands of Native Americans out of their homelands.

1845   Texas becomes a state.

1861   Abraham Lincoln is sworn in as president of the United States; the Civil War begins.

1862   Lincoln creates the Bureau of Internal Revenue within the Treasury Department.

1863   Lincoln declares slaves in the Confederacy free through the Emancipation Proclamation.

1865   The Thirteenth Amendment is added to the Constitution; President Abraham Lincoln is assassinated. Reconstruction begins.

★ ★ ★ ★ ★ ★ ★

1866 The federal government passes legislation protecting African American rights through the Freedmen's Bureau and the Civil Rights Bill.

1868 The Fourteenth Amendment is added to the Constitution.

1869 The first transcontinental railroad is completed.

1870 The Fifteenth Amendment is added to the Constitution.

1896 *Plessy v. Ferguson* is decided in the Supreme Court, upholding "separate but equal" segregation between African Americans and Caucasians.

1913 Henry Ford begins mass-producing automobiles.

1914 World War I breaks out in Europe after the assassination of Austrian Archduke Franz Ferdinand and his wife.

1918 World War I ends with the Treaty of Versailles.

1920 The Nineteenth Amendment is ratified, granting women the right to vote.

1929 Black Tuesday sees the largest stock market crash to date, triggering the Great Depression.

★ ★ ★ ★ ★ ★ ★

1939 World War II begins.

1941 Japan bombs Pearl Harbor; the United States joins World War II.

1945 World War II ends with the nuclear bombing of Japan.

1950–1953
The Korean War takes place.

1954–1975
The Vietnam War takes place.

1981 Ronald Reagan becomes president. His economic policies are dubbed "Reagonomics."

2000s The economy shifts from manufacturing to a service economy; many people move to the Sun Belt.

★ GLOSSARY ★

amendment An addition to the United States Constitution.

capitalism A political or economic system where trade and competition are controlled by private parties and not the government.

cash crop A crop raised specifically for sale rather than consumption.

colony A region or settlement outside the mother country that is controlled and ruled by that nation, usually for economic gain.

conquistadores Spanish explorers in the New World who overthrew Native American leaders and wrested control of the region.

embargo A legal ban on trade.

encomienda The Spanish caste system in the New World.

feudalism An economic system in medieval Europe in which lords owned land and peasants were required to farm it in exchange for a place to live and protection.

impress To force someone to join the army or navy.

manufacturing Turning raw materials into goods using machinery.

muckraker A nineteenth century Progressive journalist focused on social change and correcting injustice.

New Deal Government programs designed by the Roosevelt administration to alleviate and end the Great Depression.

plantation A large farm where a single cash crop was grown, often using slave labor.

tariff A tax on imports and exports.

★ FURTHER INFORMATION ★

Books

Blumenthal, Karen. *Six Days in October: The Stock Market Crash of 1929*. New York: Atheneum Books for Young Readers, 2002.

Diamond, Jared. *Guns, Germs, and Steel*. New York: W. W. Norton & Company, 2017.

DK Publishing. *The Economics Book: Big Ideas Simply Explained*. New York: Penguin, 2015.

Websites

Americans on the Move

http://amhistory.si.edu/onthemove/themes/story_47_1.html

Explore the development of different transportation modes and methods throughout American history.

AP US History Notes

https://www.apstudynotes.org/us-history

This website contains reviews and learning tools to help students understand complex topics relating to the AP US

History curriculum, including the economy and patterns of exchange.

Colonial America

http://www.smplanet.com/teaching/colonialamerica

Discover more information about a variety of topics from the colonial era, including how the United States was founded and the religions and cultures of the different colonies.

Videos

The Columbian Exchange

https://www.khanacademy.org/humanities/
ap-us-history/period-1/apush-old-and-new-
worlds-collide/v/the-columbian-exchange

This short video explains the complex exchange of animals, goods and technology, and human populations as a result of European to contact and colonization of the New World.

The History of Railroads that Tamed the West

https://www.youtube.com/watch?v=dMbq9YGxTV8

Explore the railroad boom that transformed the American West, fed manifest destiny, and changed the country forever.

★ BIBLIOGRAPHY ★

Amadeo, Kimberly. "The Great Depression: What Happened, What Caused It, How It Ended: Why There Was Only One Great Depression." *The Balance.* Last modified March 5, 2018. https://www.thebalance.com/the-great-depression-of-1929-3306033.

———. "What Was the Economy Like in the 1920s? What Made the Twenties Roar?" *The Balance.* Last modified December 22, 2017. https://www.thebalance.com/roaring-twenties-4060511.

Biography.com. "Henry Clay." Last modified April 2, 2014. https://www.biography.com/people/henry-clay-9250385.

Cornell Law School. "U.S. Constitution: 14 Amendment." Retrieved April 2, 2018. https://www.law.cornell.edu/constitution/amendmentxiv.

Crosby, Alfred W. "The Columbian Exchange: Plants, Animals, and Disease between the Old and New Worlds." Native Americans and the Land, December 2001.

http://nationalhumanitiescenter.org/tserve/nattrans/ntecoindian/essays/columbianb.htm.

Dattle, Gene. *Cotton and Race in the Making of America: The Human Costs of Economic Power*. Lanham, MD: Rowman & Littlefield Publishing Group, 2009.

Eleanor Roosevelt Papers Project. "The Progressive Era (1890–1920)." Retrieved April 2, 2018. https://www2.gwu.edu/~erpapers/teachinger/glossary/progressive-era.cfm.

Engleman, Ryan. "The Second Industrial Revolution, 1870–1914." U.S. History Scene, 2018. http://ushistoryscene.com/article/second-industrial-revolution.

Flint, Valerie I. J. "Christopher Columbus: Italian Explorer." *Encyclopedia Britannica*. Last modified January 31, 2018. https://www.britannica.com/biography/Christopher-Columbus.

Foner, Eric. "Reconstruction: United States History." *Encyclopedia Britannica*. Last modified January 5, 2018. https://www.britannica.com/event/Reconstruction-United-States-history.

Gordon, Robert J. *The Rise and Fall of the American Growth*. Princeton, NJ: Princeton University Press, 2017.

Goss, Jennifer L. "Henry Ford and the Auto Assemble Line." *ThoughtCo*, January 23, 2018. https://www.thoughtco. com/henry-ford-and-the-assembly-line-1779201.

Grady, Henry. "The American Yawp Reader: Henry Grady on the New South." *Life and Labors of Henry W. Grady, His Speeches, Writing, Etc.* Atlanta: J. C. Hudgins & Co. 1890.

Heidler, David S., and Jeanne T. Heidler. "War of 1812." *Encyclopedia Britannica.* Last modified December 13, 2017. https://www.britannica.com/event/War-of-1812.

Institute for Women's Policy Research. "Pay Equity & Discrimination." Retrieved April 2, 2018. https://iwpr.org/ issue/employment-education-economic-change/pay-equity-discrimination.

King, Gilbert. "The Woman Who Took on the Tycoon." *Smithsonian*, July 5, 2012. https://www.smithsonianmag. com/history/the-woman-who-took-on-the-tycoon-651396.

Lind, Michael. *Land of Promise: An Economic History of the United States.* New York: Harper, 2012.

Lozada, Carlos. "The Economics of World War I." National Bureau of Economic Research, January 2005. http://www.nber.org/digest/jan05/w10580.html.

McCoy, Drew R. *The Elusive Republic: Political Economy in Jeffersonian America*. Williamsburg, VA: University of North Carolina Press, 1980.

McLean, A. Torrey. "WWI: Technology and Weapons of War." *NCpedia*, 1993. https://www.ncpedia.org/wwi-technology-and-weapons-war.

Milwaukee Public Museum. "Indian Country." Retrieved April 2, 2018. http://www.mpm.edu/content/wirp/ICW-146.html.

Minster, Christopher. "The Spanish Conquistadors." *ThoughtCo*, January 12, 2018. https://www.thoughtco.com/the-spanish-conquistadors-2136564.

Morgan, Edmund S., "Columbus' Confusion About the New World." *Smithsonian*, October 2009. https://www.smithsonianmag.com/travel/columbus-confusion-about-the-new-world-140132422.

National Parks Service. "Dutch Colonies." Retrieved April 2, 2018. https://www.nps.gov/nr/travel/kingston/colonization.htm.

Nunn, Nathan, and Nancy Qian. "The Columbian Exchange: A History of Disease, Food, and Ideas." *The Journal of Economic Perspectives* 24, no. 2 (Spring 2010): 163–188.

Penobscot Marine Museum. "Navigation of American Explorers." 2012. http://penobscotmarinemuseum.org/pbho-1/history-of-navigation/navigation-american-explorers-15th-17th-centuries.

Rockoff, Hugh. "U.S. Economy in World War I." EH.net. Retrieved April 2, 2018. http://eh.net/encyclopedia/u-s-economy-in-world-war-i.

Sinclair, Upton. *The Jungle.* New York: Bantam, 1981.

Stern, Steve J. "Feudalism, Capitalism, and the World System in the Perspective of Latin America and the Caribbean." *The American Historical Review* 93, no. 4 (October 1988). pp. 829–872. http://www.jstor.org/stable/1863526.

Stewart, James I. "The Economics of American Farm Unrest, 1865-1900." EH.net. Retrieved April 2, 2018. https://eh.net/encyclopedia/the-economics-of-american-farm-unrest-1865-1900.

U.S. Department of Veteran's Affairs. "America's Wars." Retrieved April 2, 2018. https://www.va.gov/opa/publications/factsheets/fs_americas_wars.pdf.

Wood, Michael. "The Story of the Conquistadors." *BBC History*, March 29, 2011. http://www.bbc.co.uk/history/british/tudors/conquistadors_01.shtml.

★ INDEX ★

★ ABOUT THE AUTHOR ★

★ ★ ★ ★ ★ ★ ★

Cassandra Schumacher has a background in anthropology and creative writing with a focus in cultural and historical studies. She is the author of several books for young readers. Schumacher's interests are vast and varied but predominantly focus on the study of human and cultural identity throughout history into modern times. Much of her writing focuses on sociocultural interactions and power dynamics.

★ ★ ★ ★ ★ ★ ★